C000200671

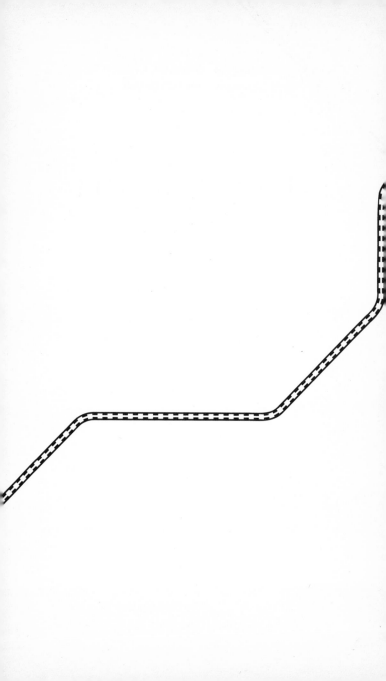

The Blue Riband

Peter York

PENGUIN BOOKS

PENGUIN BOOKS

Published by the Penguin Group
Penguin Books Ltd, 80 Strand, London WC2R ORL, England
Penguin Group (USA) Inc., 375 Hudson Street, New York, New York 10014, USA
Penguin Group (Canada), 90 Eglinton Avenue East, Suite 700, Toronto, Ontario,
Canada M4P 2Y3 (a division of Pearson Penguin Canada Inc.)
Penguin Ireland, 25 St Stephen's Green, Dublin 2, Ireland (a division of Penguin Books Ltd)
Penguin Group (Australia), 707 Collins Street, Melbourne, Victoria 3008, Australia
(a division of Pearson Australia Group Pty Ltd)
Penguin Books India Pvt Ltd, 11 Community Centre, Panchsheel Park, New Delhi – 110 017, India
Penguin Group (NZ), 67 Apollo Drive, Rosedale, Auckland 0632, New Zealand
(a division of Pearson New Zealand Ltd)
Penguin Books (South Africa) (Pty) Ltd, Block D, Rosebank Office Park, 181 Jan Smuts Avenue,
Parktown North, Gauteng 2193, South Africa

Penguin Books Ltd, Registered Offices: 80 Strand, London WC2R ORL, England

www.penguin.com

First published in Penguin Books 2013
001

Copyright © Peter York, 2013
All rights reserved

The moral right of the author has been asserted

Set in 11.75/15pt Baskerville MT Std
Typeset by Jouve (UK), Milton Keynes
Printed in England by Clays Ltd, St Ives plc

Except in the United States of America, this book is sold subject
to the condition that it shall not, by way of trade or otherwise, be lent,
re-sold, hired out, or otherwise circulated without the publisher's
prior consent in any form of binding or cover other than that in
which it is published and without a similar condition including this
condition being imposed on the subsequent purchaser

ISBN: 978-1-846-14679-4

www.greenpenguin.co.uk

MIX
Paper from
responsible sources
FSC® C018179
www.fsc.org

Penguin Books is committed to a sustainable
future for our business, our readers and our planet.
This book is made from Forest Stewardship
Council™ certified paper.

ALWAYS LEARNING   **PEARSON**

The Born-again Tubist

When I started this book I hadn't been on the Tube for twenty-five years. Or more. Very early in my working life, in my first and *only* job (in the seventies, 44 Lower Belgrave Street, next to Lord Lucan), I managed to get half a secretary – that was the word then – and access to the taxi account if I had a pretext. Over the next decade I worked up to a whole PA and unlimited taxis. I wound down my basic commutes – variously from Bayswater, Queen's Park, Sloane Square and South Ken, since you ask – over the years and became *privatized*. The man in the back of the cab.

By the mid eighties I practically never stepped on anything run by London Transport. But I *had* developed a massive working InterCity rail habit, mainly 'Go North!', plus a fortnightly trek to West Country clients, Bath or Bristol from Paddington. When clients were paying I went first class, otherwise not; my version of Keeping it Real.

So I was almost completely out of touch with the Tube. I'd missed most of the Tube's great decline – I turned over those pages in the Evening Standard – and then its nineties revival. So I was surprised to find just how *fit* most of the Tube seems now – spectacular new stations, assiduously restored old ones, clean new trains – and just how much I actually enjoyed my *rides*, as I called them.

When I started Tubing again I was like the Bateman character who asked the bus driver to take him to Sixty Eaton Square. I didn't know how to use the ticket machines and I didn't know what an Oyster card was – I thought it was like a Nectar card (call yourself a social commentator?). I didn't want to learn on the job, backing up an angry queue, so initially I bought tickets for journey X to Y at the window each time. Then my PA said that was idiotic, got me an Oyster card and everything was wonderful. *I came to love the Tube.*

In his brilliant *Underground, Overground: A Passenger's History of the Tube,* Andrew Martin describes himself as 'a person who regards a Tube journey as an end in itself'. I'm getting that way. Certainly in the first few weeks I became a positive Marie Antoinette of the Underground. I was forever telling people who turned out to have been taking the Tube five days a week over the last so many years that there was this marvellous system with conveniently placed stations everywhere you could want ('Russell Square, can you imagine!'). And you only had to slap this Oyster card thing down at either end.

I'd start retailing the last Amazing Tube Fact I'd read – about abandoned stations, deepest lines, all that – and mortifyingly learnt that practically every man I knew was a Pub Quiz Champion in Tube questions. *Everyone*, I learnt, was fascinated by the Tube, and *everyone knew more than me.* There's something there for every kind of nerd and wonk. And fogey (fogeys particularly like the Tube's inter-war Modernist architecture).

Not only that, I realized that the Piccadilly Line was special. It owned, in its central stretch, some places that'd been extraordinarily important to me but that I'd lost touch with. *Goodbye, Piccadilly, Farewell, Leicester Square.* Covent Garden and Earl's Court too. I'd go round them or near them now but not quite *to* them any more. And I'd be going for different reasons. To BAFTA or to a blockbuster opening at the RA, to Jermyn Street – *I never shook that habit* – but not to the Circus itself. Not the Dilly, not Eros, none of that. And not the giant first-run Leicester Square cinemas or the lovely vanishing cheap food places all round it.

Covent Garden too, an absolute centre of my world from about '75 – the opening of Zanzibar in Great Queen Street, Blitz further down the road in the early eighties – to '85, the opening of the Groucho Club in Dean Street. Or South Ken and Gloucester Road. I was there from '79 to '89 – I lived about equidistant from the two stations but almost always went to South Ken. South Ken/Gloucester Road/Earl's Court and Baron's Court had all been *material* over that decade because so many of the happy tribal sterotypes I wrote about – Sloanes and Mercs and Thems – lived in those stucco cliffs (but not so much in the next-along bourgeois bits of Hammersmith, which like, say, Barnes, is somehow more 'Home Counties' than deep London).

Once I started on my Tube crawl round the Piccadilly Line's fifty stations – the minimum foray was up to the main concourse, one phone photograph, façade ditto, down nearest high street, talk to estate agent, get house details – I realized the Piccadilly Line station was often the most interesting thing about the place. It's the escape route, the embassy of Modernity,

5

the outward and visible symbol of an inner world completely different from the overground suburb or the bleak transitional stretches of, say, Caledonian Road.

And the most thought-through too. My clever, economic-history, know-all friends have pointed out the ramshackle entrepreneurial origins of the Tube network – so many companies, so little master planning, so different from Paris or Moscow. No Haussmann above or below. But my design and architecture ones all know how it came together so brilliantly later, with what American fundamentalists call Intelligent Design. The Tube was so much more than the sum of its parts.

Anyone expecting all fifty-three Piccadilly Line stations – actually four serve Heathrow so they don't count – and their hinterlands to be covered here will be disappointed. Other books exist for that, masses of them. There are Tube porn books with photographs of every Tube station going. There are books about every Tube station *ever*, dead or alive.

All by men. (Down Street, Mayfair and Aldwych/ Strand are famous ghost stations from the early Piccadilly Line development.) David Leboff, who works for Transport for London, has written reams on the Tube stations and could clearly win *Mastermind* on the subject. And sociologists – real ones – have written depressing reports on the decline of the more 'ordinary' inter-war suburbs, the kind the Piccadilly Line goes through to reach Cockfosters, Uxbridge or Heathrow.

Instead I've focussed much more narrowly on just some of the central places on the line that I know. Places so singular or important they define the line and its character, rather than the other way around. Green Park is at the very centre of Piccadilly world – Mayfair out of the North entrance, St James's to the South. It's Ancient and Modern. Knightsbridge is the centre of a new Global Plutocrat culture. South Ken is central to a certain kind of English life, one the French have bought into. All of them places so apparently familiar

and touristic, so *gazetteered* that, if you live in
Big London, you're constantly surprised to
realize friends in Muswell Hill or Shepherd's
Bush – serious types who don't get out in luxury
land – have lost touch with the extraordinary
changes in these places over the last ten to
fifteen years (I'm thinking patronisingly about
lovely people at the BBC or the *Guardian* here).

When I say I *know* these places it's because
I've either lived there (or nearly), worked
there – or just hung around there when I did
a lot of that. Or I've got spies there. So I think
I recognize the tribal signs in those areas – the
smells and the textures. I know the look of the
people – the percentage of Richard James to
Paul Smith suits by postcode. I know the look of
their houses, the uptake of easy contemporary
art and Hamilton Gallery Big Photographs
within packaged interiors, just by house type.
It's my sort of thing.

The Piccadilly Line, *at its original core*, is full
of my sort of thing. So when it comes to tough
choices, I've chosen not to ferret out the latter-day

Abigail's Party stories down the suburban line. Or the Mary Portas ones – though the high streets around those suburban Tube stations are changing at a lick. I've spent thousands of hours in suburbs around the UK and around the world, interviewing people, conducting *focus groups* and listening to other people conduct them (simultaneous translation). I *love* good suburbs, but it's too much like work.

In any case, I'm beginning to think the place I like best is *the Tube itself.* There are novels like Keith Lowe's *Tunnel Vision*, about people spending a day or a Flying-Dutchman lifetime on the Tube, driven by the ancient literary idea that it's a living hell. But not for me. Give me an iPad and a notebook – kind Richard Branson has been WiFi-ing up the Tube recently – and I'd happily pootle around all day.

I've been getting bolder. I branched out from the Piccadilly Line. I tried to work out how to go to lunch on the Tube, or *to* a party (if it was late or I felt whacked I still did the *from* with an account-taxi home). In a few

9

weeks I was on the Tube practically every day, which meant catching up with my early life. *But feeling quite different about it.* The Tube had been unquestioned, always there, its structures and textures, noises and smells, its reds, greens and creams, its 'moquette' fabrics on the seats, were things I'd known forever. I'd seen it as a London child with my mother and her sisters – even with my grandmother (my father didn't trust it; he felt safer in his car). There'd *always* been a Tube where we lived. In Hampstead, most local rumbling and subsidence was attributed to it. And the point of the Tube for me then, in London NW, was always that you were going *further in* – to the very centre. And *underground*. It was almost never about clattering out overground to an outer suburb. I liked being *impelled* inwards by a benign force and an anonymous crowd.

But *going back*, everything about the Tube's subterranean world struck me as extraordinary. Quite unnatural in the best possible way, with its logic, order and *flow*. Its complete contrast to the ramshackle madness of overground London. The Good Design simplicity of almost everything (of course there are idiotic sixties and seventies tiling moments, but the basics go from good to great). I found myself thinking the Tube was *a Modernist experiment that'd worked.*

I began to look forward to my Tube trips. Anywhere to anywhere. The look of everything and the great windy swirl of it. The delicious gold-plating of the information, where you saw and heard exactly where you were going every two minutes or so. And that nice voice, the completely English, RP, contralto-ish, Radio-4 sort of voice, *would even tell you about the connections* you could get at each station ('Change here for the Northern Line'). It's all terribly rational.

Part of my own vaguely remembered romance-of-the-Tube had always been that it was nicely classless, compared with the world overground. No first- and second-class carriages. And all human life was there, an unpredictable mixture, enjoying the Utopian

Modernist Experience. But going back tells you the Tube is a relatively middle-class experience, and a dig tells you it always has been. London's bottom tenth, the poorest, unluckiest, most sink-estate people don't usually go on the Tube. People on the minimum wage or none usually work near home or stay close to it. They see the Tube as *expensive* and somehow intimidating. London's army of office cleaners from everywhere usually goes on the buses.

But for *mobile* people with a commute and a dream, the Tube is liberating and affordable. You see students from everywhere, and tourists from everywhere. In the centre the Piccadilly has *more key attractions* than any other line. The Tube is *deeply* aspirational.

My own aspirations have always been uptown, top-ranking ones; my own version of the *urban dream*. In my teens, for instance, I thought I'd like a flat above a shop in one of those Edwardian red-brick blocks around the Charing Cross Road (Leicester Square Tube). Nightlife, bookshops and cheap cafés.

I've never really longed for the West Village
loft or the artist's redeemed industrial slum,
I never wanted anywhere particularly *vibrant*
(airhead euphemism for borderline ghetto-
ish) or 'edgy' (safe proximity of law-breakers).
I wanted the real early twentieth-century city
centre, part-commercial, part residential.
Living above a shop. The alienation of *The
Lonely Crowd* was not a problem in this teenage
dream. 'Downtown . . . everything's waiting for
you.' It was obvious that Pet Clark wasn't on
about . . . *Shoreditch*, or the West Village, Brixton
or the South Bronx, *she meant Piccadilly Circus*
('Linger on the sidewalk where the neon lights
are pretty').

I'm so design-aware now it hurts. I've seen
the Futurists and the Marinetti Manifesto.
I know the route from Bauhaus to Our House,
from Modernist to Moderne. I can see why
my architecture and design friends are always
on about the Tube; about the Map, *Beck's
map*, which is a constant of those Top Ten
Graphic Design lists; about suburban stations'

architecture, and particularly about *Arnos Grove* – I'd never been there till 2012. And about Frank Pick and the *design management* history of the Tube. But design management was a new bit of corporate-speak I only learnt back when I was weaning myself *off* the Tube.

I liked it for precisely that capital M for Modernist vibe I hadn't understood before. The Tube, whatever its earlier shortcomings – being boiled, having to stand, a bit shabby in parts, though never as smelly as people said – was the Future that really worked (and for the many, not the few, to use a Blair-ism). Affordable, efficient, classless-*seeming*. *It's everything upstairs London isn't.* Someone was saying on TV recently how London's poorest shopping streets were lined with Chicken Cottages, mini-marts, pound shops and betting shops. But their subterranean Tube platforms don't reflect any of that; the Tube brings its middle-class, slightly nanny-state design values *everywhere* it goes. It could be Waitrose, with its partners and policies.

The deep Tube aesthetic *is* distinctive, a

more International Style than most of London. By 1906, when the Piccadilly Line opened, the Tube was mainly *electric*. It needed American and European help; a lot of the first technology, from electric motors to deep drilling machines, was bought in. (British Imperial overground trains were chuffing around, Stevenson-style, well into the sixties.) The first, late-Victorian phase of the Underground – from 1863 to the 1890s – had itself been about comic-looking chuffers in shallow 'cut-and-cover' tunnels. They look as if they were sulphurous hell to travel on, and there's a lot of Victorian writing to confirm it. The truth is that, although Brits may have been first to put trains in tunnels, the *real* deep Tube, like so many key technologies of the modern world, was actually an Edwardian roll-out, a contemporary of the Paris Métro and the New York subway. So my Modernist/ Internationalist fantasy wasn't that fanciful after all.

There's a well-subscribed cult around Tube design. If you're a proper Tube geek you recognize the historic and technical differences in different places, on different lines. And the different *rolling stock*. (I realize now that the 'classic' Tube trains I went on in the sixties and seventies will, some of them, actually have been made in the late thirties.) The nerds know their types and series, but, for me, flicking through the pictures right back to the first Edwardian electric trains, they *all* look pretty modern, inside and out. They're from a different century compared with their contemporary, the overground steam train. Their low, red snakiness is apparent early on and it's beautiful.

The Tube's aesthetics deserve attention because they're so important: the Tube was once at the centre of British arts politics. My vague intimations of the Tube as an historic Modernist Project were completely right. I'd taken to describing myself – amusingly, I thought – as a Tubist, and then I found the word had really been part of the twenties intelligentsia's vocabulary – as a play on Cubist.

This story is all about more than just some

exemplary Design Management. The Tube, its twenties and thirties MD, Frank Pick, and his arts patronage were at the absolute centre of the style wars. At some point, Pick, the solicitor from Spalding, the management trainee who was considered good at statistics, started to morph into a man with a mission about Good Modern Design. At first there was the communication alibi – that good design attracted attention. Then it moved into an altogether more zealous phase, one where Pick was forever on platforms, telling anyone who'd listen that good design was fundamental to what MBAs now call the corporate brand. And he became very directly involved in the company's choice of architects, artists and designers. He took on the roles we'd call marketing director, advertising manager and public affairs director precisely as he was rising to the top in central management (becoming CEO and Vice Chairman). And then he became a sort of one-man Design Council. He was president of the Design and Industries Association and the

17

first chairman of the Council for Art & Industry in the thirties. The Transport Museum archive has reams of Pick's speeches and position papers on design and urban planning. He was central to the struggle for 'ownership' of the visual arts in Britain between the wars. In a period when the major European developments barely got a look-in in Britain, when Academicians denounced European Modern Art from the pulpit of the RA, *the Tube was London's new museum of modern art.* It gave *modern* architects, artists and designers a new, vastly bigger audience through stations, advertising, the maps and trains themselves. And a *Tubist* was a popular Modernist.

Behind all this lay the between-wars debate about Britain's future, about the nature of British art and its relationship to the fiendish European avant-garde. And politics. Back then Frank Pick had been centre stage in the battle as a leading . . . *Medieval Modernist.* According to Michael Saler, Professor of History at the University of California, Davis, one of those

American academics who knows us better
than we do ourselves, Medieval Modernists
were an important group of influential
British arts patrons, curators, collectors and
administrators operating in the first half of the
twentieth century.* They were typically born
in the late nineteenth century, outsiders, often
Northern and Non-conformist, brought up on
Ruskin and Morris (the 'medieval' grounding).
They then developed into proselytizers for a
particularly English kind of Modernism in
the early twentieth century. A toned-down,
commercially practical, socially useful, *improving*
kind. A nanny state, mixed-economy kind. The
opposite of those Bloomsbury 'Art for Itself'
Formalists, Roger Fry and Clive Bell, with their
effetely un-English attitudes. And both, of
course, a mile away from the *Daily Express* Little
Englander views on any European design.

Funny, forgotten, uptight Frank Pick, MD

* *The Avant-Garde in Interwar England: Medieval Modernism
and the London Underground* (2001).

of the Tube, was central to English cultural politics then: through his patronage of a group of modern fine artists, like sculptors Henry Moore, Eric Gill and Jacob Epstein, who otherwise wouldn't have reached a mass audience (the rude Epstein sculpture on Charles Holden's 1928 London Transport Westminster headquarters was especially controversial. Protests forced a swift stonemason's penis reduction). It's difficult to think of a figure in public life with a remotely comparable role now. Sir Nicholas Serota of the Tate crossed with Sir Stuart Rose, perhaps, if Rose had decided to turn all the M&S stores over to contemporary art shows when he was in charge of the company. Anyway, there was the Tube, centre stage, battling for your granny's artistic soul. Nikolaus Pevsner, in his *Art, Architecture and Design: Victorian and After*, said of Pick: 'He was, to add a last word, the greatest patron of the arts whom this century has so far produced in England, and indeed the ideal patron of our age.' Ernest Turner, in his *Shocking History of*

Advertising, made an extravagant comparison, describing Pick as 'the nearest approach to Lorenzo the Magnificent that a modern democracy can achieve'.

Frank Pick died in 1941. After the war the Medieval Modernists, Pick, the curator William Rothenstein and the critic Herbert Read, were either dead or hopelessly unfashionable – and forgotten by the sixties. But, in 1978, interest in Pick and the between-wars Tube revived dramatically with a V&A exhibition on his patronage, 'Teaspoons and Trains' . Those Charles Holden tube station buildings are mainly listed buildings and are endlessly photographed now, the Underground posters are constantly revived and reproduced – the Underground Map is one of the most admired graphics in the universe and the whole Frank Pick achievement is seen as *a homily about our National Character.*

The key architects of that pre-war Tube-station Look were Leslie Green and Charles Holden. Green did the Edwardian stations on the first stretch of the Piccadilly. (He also designed my childhood station, Hampstead, on the Northern Line, in 1907, and Belsize Park and Chalk Farm nearby). They had his characteristic first-floor arched windows and glazed, liver-coloured faience tiles.

But the real glory of the architectural Grand Design for the Tube came later, starting in the early thirties. It was further out too, when the Piccadilly Line was extended from Finsbury Park to Cockfosters in the North-east and Uxbridge in the West. The Tube's definitive inter-war architect, Charles Holden, built a line of stations that were *embassies of Modernism*. They carried a message to rough working-class areas and suburbs built in Tudorbethan and pebble-dash Bypass Variegated alike. If you wanted the symbolism of a newer world, Charles Holden was making those shapes against the sky. The shapes and styles he and Frank Pick had seen in their tours of Northern Europe's New Architecture in the late twenties.

Pick and Holden, an odd uptight couple of

Northern Quakers, reported back on Modernist buildings in Germany and Sweden. They saw Weimar and Stockholm, and they brought them to suburban London. From Bauhaus to Manor House. Holden's key Modernist Tube stations were in undistinguished outer suburbs, because only in those developing areas could you work practically from scratch. In Central London Tube stations had to fit in physically and stylistically with their cramped, important surroundings. There, they might have stone-clad frontages and more conventional fenestration forced on them. But in most of the suburban locations they could go for broke.

The Piccadilly Line has more of Charles Holden's Modernist inter-war stations than any other line, as every design-literate type but me has known forever: the only coherent group of home-grown English Modernist public buildings of its period in London. There are twenty-four of them actually, more than on all the other lines put together, famous and referenced in architecture schools. *Fourteen* of them are listed. The Holden stations are the outward and enduring symbols of that great inter-war arts battle.

Out There – how to say this nicely? – there's practically an inverse relationship between the distinction of the area and the singularity of the Piccadilly Line station. What else can you tell me about Arnos Grove? The Holden drum (1933) is the defining logo for this otherwise low-wattage area (like the Chermayeff De La Warr Pavilion for dull Bexhill). And the escape route out of it.

The stations were the only really Modernist buildings for miles. Between the wars architectural Modernism was endlessly discussed but not much built in Britain. There'd been a little in those untypical villages, Hampstead and Highgate, designed by European refugees on their way to America, and a fair bit of cod Deco and Moderne in suburban cinemas and seaside villas. So to commission the Holden stations – even toned down and Anglicized as they were by a more modest scale and russet-brick outer skins – was decidedly brave of Frank Pick.

For people in the thirties suburbs, those new Tube stations must've been as exciting as if a flying saucer had landed on their town. There's a famous photograph of Charles Holden's 1933 Grade II*-listed Southgate Tube, *all lit up* at night, glowing like a sci-fi apparition. Around it – if you've done Southgate like me, you'll know – are Englishmen's Castles, contemporary small semis so Edwardian-looking they could've been designed in 1910. Those stations must have been fantastically aspirational, with a message as clear as that old Harrods advertising line 'Enter a different world'. The thirties Tube was modern, glamorous and clever, *a metaphor for a new world.*

The Blue Riband

When I lived in Marylebone, near Marble Arch,
I always used to say I lived 'at the centre of the
world'. It *was* brilliantly located for practically
everything there. But I knew perfectly well I'd
stolen the line from Piccadilly Circus. Piccadilly
Circus, at the very end of the nineteenth
century, after several reconstructions and the
installation of Alfred Gilbert's aluminium Eros,
with the fountain and steps below, was *officially*
the centre of the world. It was the village green
of the largest empire ever known, ruled over
by the dumpy Queen Empress just along at the
end of the Mall.

If you pore over the picture postcards (they were conveniently invented in *1894*, the year after Eros went up) collected in David Oxford's little book *Piccadilly Circus* you see that, in a typically British way, *it was never all that.* Scale, planning and architectural quality all look completely pony and ramshackle compared with any triumphalist Euro-capital of the period. Berlin, Vienna – but especially Paris. The London Pavilion, the only surviving Victorian façade in the Circus (1885), was a purpose-built variety theatre with the look of a giant boozer with cod-classical aspirations. The stylistic connection with Nash's Great Curve of Regent Street was lost early on. All that remains of the notional quadrant is the former Swan and Edgar corner building, rebuilt in the twenties.

And from the very first pictures on, the Circus is *wildly commercial!* With everything advertised to everybody in the most unregulated, *unedited* way. The horse-drawn buses are advertising hit shows – Shaftsbury Avenue had been built in 1885 – the Pavilion itself is advertising German beer (later of course, there was a wall of illuminated signs next to it). It will have looked utterly garish to a sophisticated European eye. None of that mattered because it wasn't built for glory, but for business – retail, entertainment, catering, sex – and so nothing is sacred, part of a Grand Design. It's changing all the time, reflecting new entertainment and new technology. After the Second World War it becomes a sort of miniature Times Square, where the neon advertising has become an attraction in itself.

By 1906 the first Piccadilly Line Tube station was up and running in the Circus, part of the original stretch (from Hammersmith to Finsbury Park). It was set into an existing Victorian building (later rebuilt and 'façaded') with a wide blue fascia running across between the ground and first floors. It wasn't the station we know, but an Edwardian affair, with the Leslie Green look. Leslie Green was the architect-designer for the Piccadilly Line entrepreneur Charles Yerkes.

The Piccadilly Circus station we know now is a marvel. It's a lovely underground Deco drum lined out in travertine marble, all detailed in bronze. It replaced the Leslie Green one in 1928 and was seen as an astounding Modernist flagship. But nobody really looks any more. It's just faintly shabby; the floor looks like a replacement. It's slightly underlit. And the shops and concessions – original in their time – look like painful survivals. But just think how it will have looked to its first users. Anyone up West then will have recognized the style as like something *out of the American movies*, where the designers borrowed freely from that European look that said Modern Luxury. Or from the new illustrated magazines that showed the Houses of the Stars.

In 1928 Piccadilly Circus Station stood for Things to Come. The drum concourse and the original escalators with their reeded bronze column uplighters will have said The Future as clearly as the vast Jubilee Line extension steel-and-glass cathedrals of 1999 do now.

When I was first going up West to Piccadilly I vaguely knew it was something I might just have called Deco. But I wouldn't have stopped to look. I didn't have the design vocabulary, I wouldn't have known the materials, the references. And I certainly wouldn't have known about *Holden*, Charles Holden, its architect.

Charles Saumarez Smith, Chief Executive of the Royal Academy, pointed out to me that the glory of Charles Holden's 1928 Piccadilly Circus Station underground concourse could happily sit under Holden's famous overground Arnos Grove station of 1933. The same drum shape and dramatic Modern-for-the-People styling. For Saumarez Smith the four station exits on the Piccadilly 'quadrant' – it isn't really one now – give on to four different kinds of London. Shaftesbury Avenue is old (1885), middle-class theatreland, now with its High-Concept big hits and imported stars. The Haymarket and Lower Regent Street exits give on to Old Establishment London from St James's down to Buckingham Palace and

Whitehall. Regent Street is nineteenth-century, middlebrow shopping; while Piccadilly itself marks the line between St James's, where the Ruling Class did their serious work of running the show, and Mayfair, where they had houses and whores. It's Burlington Bertie's – the musical half-fictional toff – great parade ground. Grand London's central artery.

Piccadilly itself, as Saumarez Smith points out, is oddly disappointing. It's a long, wide, straight historic road lined with masses of hugely important buildings – and the ghosts of others, now demolished. Some are important for what goes on there, some for their architecture, many for both. It ranges from Wren's St James's Church and the former In and Out Club, once Palmerston's house, to BAFTA's rather Deco-ish spaces. It's got Fortnum and Mason's marvellously detailed, Gainsborough-Films-Georgian store of 1926 and Hatchards' 1909 rebuild of its original 1797 site. There's a giant Waterstones bookshop in what was originally the Simpson clothing palace, built in the most elegant restrained Euro-Modernist way for Dr Simpson in 1935 (lots of travertine marble echoing the station concourse below. It makes the High Street Kensington Deco-ish stores look pretty crass and overweight.)

Further up there's the London Ritz, opened in 1907. It's steel-framed, custom-built for twentieth-century modern luxury, but completely clad in Beaux Arts stone, the interior the definitive version of that Fancy French style, so distinctive that in 1909 the American art historian Bernard Berenson described the seamless world of the international rich as 'Ritzonia': 'Ritzonia, carries its inmates like a wishing carpet from place to place, the same people, the same meals, the same music. Within its walls you might be at Peking or Prague or Paris or London and you would never know where.'

Across Bury Street from the Ritz there's Chris Corbin and Jeremy King's The Wolseley, a perpetually smart restaurant in a perfect fantasy twenties building. A restaurant that's become, in just one decade, another centre of the world. Jeremy King told me that 'Green Park is a transport hub. The Mayfair money men come here for breakfast – the earliest sitting – then they go on to Canary Wharf by Tube. The fashion-and-PR "ladies who breakfast" come later. Roger Katz from Hatchards told us that we'd changed our stretch of Piccadilly – he said we'd given people a reason to come back here. The Wolseley was a car showroom. There's a line in Anthony Powell's *A Dance to the Music of Time* where someone says "He's just gone down to Piccadilly to buy a Bentley".' Oliver Peyton, caterer to the Thinking Classes with his cafés and restaurants in the National Gallery, the Wallace Collection, Heals and the Royal Academy, says: 'Piccadilly's still got a bit of allure. It still retains a sense of London-ness – much of Mayfair is a foreign country now. There's always somewhere to go round here, a seedy basement club, something. The Gents in Piccadilly Circus was always famous for cottaging. My gay staff were always going there. And till recently there was that famous Formica Café behind the Circus. There's a lot of good seedy history there. The Regent Palace Hotel rented rooms by the hour.'

The most important, most defining visitor attraction in Piccadilly is the Royal Academy. The high Victorian front of 1873 is stuck on to Lord Burlington's original house of 1718. It has that vast-for-London courtyard, those wings with learned societies. It puts on blockbuster exhibitions. Its great season-opening middlebrow pot-boiler Summer Exhibition runs from June to August. And it's in an exciting growth spurt now, combining the front and the 'back' (the old Museum of Mankind in Burlington Gardens). Or there's the Albany, a sort of Regency apartment block reworked in 1802 from Prince Frederick, Duke of York and Albany's London house. It's sublimely haut-fogey with its 'sets' and its precious tenants (in about 1990 I seriously considered buying a big Albany set with a view down Savile Row. It cost about double a comparable flat in, say, South Ken.

Friends teased me out of it; I wasn't old enough or fogey-precious enough to live in a museum. I am now).

Anyway, the Saumarez-Smith point is that with all this – and there's masses more – *Piccadilly the street feels still oddly less than the sum of its parts*. It's not a Grand Allée now, a big architectural conception, like Portland Place or The Mall, nor a high Victorian parade of class confidence, like Pall Mall. It's not exactly where the toffs live. And it doesn't feel that lively; they don't open flagships there.

The best Piccadilly buildings – the RA, St James's, the Albany – are all *set back* from the street. It doesn't hold together; it's too big and too varied. Too trafficked and bus-laned. While street histories are popular book and TV subjects, there's been no big book about Piccadilly since about 1920.* It's got sublimely

---

* In his *London: The Biography*, Peter Ackroyd gives Piccadilly about a page, and then it's only about the Circus and the sex; boys and girls having adventures

useful access to extraordinary places – the
Piccadilly Line runs under the street from
Piccadilly Circus to Hyde Park Corner via
Green Park. There are three stops on the
same line on one street – and it's stuffed with
history – but the Edwardian heart's gone
out of it.

The Piccadilly Line was officially opened
by David Lloyd George, then President of the
Board of Trade in Campbell-Bannerman's
Liberal Government, on Saturday, 15 December
1906. Lloyd George rode the length of the
Great Northern Piccadilly and Brompton
Railway (GNP&BR), its mouthful name
until 1928, from Hammersmith to Finsbury
Park. At the opening lunch in the singular,
Victorian-exotic gold-mosaiced (1874) Criterion
Restaurant on Piccadilly Circus (still there,
restored and revived like the neighbouring

---

and selling their bodies. And he's only got a line each for
Jermyn Street and Mayfair – more whores – and nothing
at all for St James's. He *is* a funny one.

Criterion Theatre), Lloyd George commended the new line for being *electric* (we were behind the US and Europe in the number of electrically powered passenger miles travelled here, he said) and for being an example of co-operation between private enterprise and the great municipal authority of London. Lloyd George was right to worry about Britain falling behind technically and industrially. And that was a bit of mixed-economy thinking before its time; the Tube joined the public sector in 1933 as the London Passenger Transport Board.

The new Piccadilly Line had freebooting capitalist origins. It was part of the gloriously Edwardian-sounding Underground Electric Railways Company, by then the leading business in underground development. The UERC had already launched two other new-generation, deep-tunnelled, electric-powered Tube lines that year, elaborately named ones that later became the Northern Line and the Bakerloo Line. The UERC had been assembled in a series of takeovers by Charles Tyson Yerkes

(1837–1905), American Master of the Universe and transatlantic commuter, using advanced financial engineering and – mainly – American shareholders' money. They brought in new European and American technology for the engines, rolling stock and deep-tunnelling machines. And they built the giant Lots Road Power Station by the river in Chelsea in 1905 to supply the electricity.

The original Piccadilly Line proposal was *for a short, sweet and very smart line.* It would take people from South Kensington Station, serving the late 1860s Italianate stucco cliffs of the South Kensington development, up through Knightsbridge and Mayfair to Piccadilly Circus, the centre of the Known World. It'd been conceived by one of the businesses Charles Yerkes had taken over, the Brompton and Piccadilly. Once in the Yerkes combine, the proposal was bigged up in 1901 by merging it with another Yerkes acquisition, the Great Northern and Strand Railway. It was extended to Hammersmith in the West, and to Finsbury

Park, a growing Pooterville junction to the North-east, with a spur from Holborn to the Strand (for the theatre traffic) opened in 1907.

For me, the core proposition of the pre-merger Piccadilly Plan – the heart of it – remained about *moving smart people to nice places*. There was more to the economic rationale of course: the South Kensington to Piccadilly line filled a gap in the network. Piccadilly was originally a Bakerloo Line station, and South Kensington had been part of the Mark 1, 1860s, Metropolitan, steam Underground set-up, trains running in shallow 'cut and cover' tunnels. The new line pulled them together usefully, connecting North, South and West.

The Northern extension was a mixed blessing. It ran on to Leicester Square and Covent Garden – then very much the *Pygmalion* flower and produce market – then through mid-town Holborn, home of insurance companies and growing law firms, the dull heavy lifting of the Edwardian financial empire, to Bloomsbury's Russell Square, for the British Museum and the growing university. Then it went on to King's Cross: the King's Cross hinterland was always grim, if you look at Henry Mayhew's nineteenth-century social-geography map of London streets. The stations that followed weren't exactly peachy either. Caledonian Road for Pentonville Prison, Holloway Road for the working-class bustle and the immigrants, on to Arsenal (originally Gillespie Road) and Finsbury Park, where tram and overground connections took early commuters out into the growing north-east suburbs.

The two stretches – Finsbury Park to King's Cross and Piccadilly to South Ken – were practically Disraeli's Two Nations. Piccadilly itself at that point was still obviously the grandees' Grande Allée, with Devonshire House, the Duke of Devonshire's massive London house opposite Green Park (demolished for a block of flats in 1924) and many more toff town houses besides. Clubmen still ruled an empire – or thought they did – from St James's: the Spencers were still in Spencer House;

the Duke of Sutherland was still in Stafford House – now the Government hospitality joint Lancaster House – the massive house, where Queen Victoria, on a neighbourly visit from just up the road, said, 'I have come from my house to your palace.' Marlborough House, built by Wren and his son for the Marlboroughs, was still a royal overflow palace. (Edward VII and Alexandra had lived there before he succeeded in 1901.)

Piccadilly gave on to two of the grandest areas in London. Even now the updated, 2003 Pevsner,* hardly excitable, says of St James's: 'The houses of this select area include some marvels.' In St James's, the royal palaces – Buckingham and St James's – are the least of it. Hermione Hobhouse's *Lost London* gives you some idea of how stuffed with Grade-I*-plus-plus architecture Piccadilly itself, Mayfair and St James were before the First World War.

The Piccadilly Line is the tourist trophy

* *The Buildings of England: London 6: Westminster*, Simon Bradley and Nikolaus Pevsner.

line. Transport for London's Consumer Insight
Manager, Ian Pring, told me that the Piccadilly
Line had significantly more tourists than other
lines – it's got Heathrow at one end, after all.
Other Tube lines do useful and interesting
things. The Central takes the investment
banking population of Holland Park and
Notting Hill to the City. The Circle circulates
past some smart places – Heavy Kensington,
W8, Sloane Square and then Westminster. But
the Piccadilly simply has more *trophies* on its
original route than any other line. More A-List
Tourist Attractions: South Ken for the museums;
Knightsbridge for Harrods and the rest; Green
Park for the Royal Palaces; Piccadilly Circus
and Leicester Square for a night out up West,
in every guidebook for 150 years. Covent
Garden, long after the smarties left it, remains
a massive draw for young tourists – it's huge in
Japan, big in Beijing; Russell Square for the
British Museum and its six million visitors a
year (Holborn is equidistant, but it's boring.
Russell Square is Bloomsbury proper.) They're

all *organized*, street-signed, stacked with those especially tacky yet dull British souvenir shops. And yet all quite incontrovertibly *world class*.

The Piccadilly Line is the hyper-money line too. The houses and flats around that original South Ken to Piccadilly stretch are some of the most expensive in the world ('prestigious' is the tacky estate-agent speak for them). Mayfair, St James's (St James's is mainly flats and not many of them, but the price per square foot is still shooting up) and Knightsbridge/Belgravia with its painfully 'bling' new Global money, are *Super-Prime*. South Ken and Gloucester Road are Prime, full of four-million-pound flats and pushing-ten-million-pound houses, now churning with runaway Euro-trash. Plus Bloomsbury and Earl's Court, differently wrecked, but with massively charming class-correct, borderline Prime pockets – where three- to four-million-pound flats are quite common now. The centre of the Piccadilly Line, in other words, runs through where the other half lives.

It's all wrapped in the dark-blue ribbon
of the Piccadilly Line livery on the famous
map. It's the colour of pony-club prizes and
Tory rosettes. The Blue Riband, the Gordon
Blue (Cordon Bleu). If the line's most central
stations were a group of hotels, they'd call it
an 'upmarket collection', like the old Savoy
Group. The areas round the core stretch of
the Piccadilly have money and *cultural capital* in
spades.

Boiling Mayfair

It's boiling in Mayfair now. It's particularly hot on the Piccadilly side – rather than the Oxford Street one – and in the part served by the unremarkable-looking Green Park Station, rather than Piccadilly or Hyde Park Corner. It's boiling in money, there's a complete *moronic inferno* (little Martin Amis has his moments), involving the global super rich and the people who serve them. Let's hear it for Ukrainian trophy wives. Sometimes the people who serve them are super-rich too. They never get to be less than hyper-rewarded by our little British standards.

Flight Capital, big runaway money from dodgy dangerous places, is a major part of it. The recent runaway rich from the Arab Spring and the Euro meltdown have compounded the overheating in Mayfair, pushing it from hot to a rolling boil. If London's a safe haven for these super-rich refugees, then they'll go to famous, familiar places. You won't get Golden Greeks and Milanese Moneybags setting up in Shoreditch or Stoke Newington. That's why Prime Central London is so like Hounslow Central; they're both so vibrantly multicultural, darling.

The super-rich – the global *serious money* people – come from absolutely everywhere to live, work and trade in twenty-first-century Mayfair. *As house buyers*, they particularly come from Western Europe, Eastern Europe and the Middle East, according to estate agent Savills' research about the buyers of Prime property (average price £3 million), Super Prime (£6.5 million) and Ultra Prime (£15 million on average). They're usually often absentees. The primest houses and flats in Mayfair's new

Super-prime developments are, according to Yolanda Barnes, Savills' Head of Research, bought almost entirely by non-doms, the Rich List euphemism for *foreigners*. The tiny clutch of Brits in at that level are really non-doms too, defined by their tax status and time spent in their various houses and offices around the world. They're lost to us.

Then there are the money men. The other overlapping *players* in the Great Game of New Mayfair plutocracy are people who work in Mayfair/St James's huge but secretive finance sector. Mayfair is the world's 'second City' of hedge funds, private equity firms and 'family offices'. But unlike the Square Mile, with its familiar names, its huge purpose-built eighties-on-steroids *corporate* buildings, its giant atria with those obvious corporate art collections, the Mayfair City is discreet. There are, according to my spies, more than 500 businesses in Mayfair money land, but with relatively small workforces – a couple of hundred at most, most of them with five to twenty people all up.

They're not exactly working in shacks, but because there's been very little high-drama development of the Shard kind – giant sites boarded up for miles, towering cranes, all that – Mayfair has been utterly transformed on a rather quiet basis over the last fifteen years. Little companies have floors in anonymous, upgraded blocks. Some work behind hollowed-out Georgian façades with built-out, built-on backs, 40-foot rooms where you least expect them. *And always with the newest kit.*

This is where intimidatingly clever young men – it *is* overwhelmingly men, and young, they can't hack it much after forty – use spectacular computer power to do things incredibly *fast*. They're people who will, most of them, have started in the clunky old City, and been drawn here with transfer fees and the promise of being that much *closer* to the money. Unlike the City, which is show-off and secretive by turn, this world is constantly and constitutionally secretive. They don't advertise. They don't need strings of public-affairs people and sponsorship programmes at the RA up the road, like big banks. They don't have that many *stakeholders* who remotely matter to them. *Most people don't know they're there.* They're like sportsmen working to their peak, offsite, or – the more popular comparison – gamblers. But gamblers with a system and an infrastructure of super-fast computers, all hanging on the heartbeat of every important 'feed' – from the various stock exchanges, the Bank of England, the everything, all crammed with instructions – if this, do that – digital betting where a millisecond's advantage can make billions.

The Mayfair hedge fund industry is Europe's largest by a mile. Yet no one, so it seems, has really mapped it for laymen, profiled the firms, looked at who owns them, and from where, who works in them (my friends say it's about 30 per cent Brit managers and 70 per cent everyone else), what their rewards look like and what they mean for the area, for London and for the country more generally. You'd think at least one of the one hundred or so departments of sociology in British universities would have looked up from studying Transgressive Transsexuals in Thamesmead for a moment to raise some grant-funding to look at how this fantastically important culture actually operates.

Hedge-fund guys, for all their Richard James bespoke, Regency Buck suits, are actually monastic madmen. A friend tells me he has a *replica computer kit* – a wraparound wall of screens reporting the world just like the one in his Curzon Street office – in a walk-through study next to his bedroom at home in South Ken. He wants to follow things in real time into the night. The distress of Hedge-fund Wives is legendary: they've lost their men to a force as absolute as fanatical religion or the military. The same spy says they often have weepy girly drinks at San Lorenzo, one of Saint Diana's favourite restaurants, in Beauchamp Place. There are compensations. Made-it hedge-funders like Crispin Odey and

Alan Howard feature on the high stretches of *The Sunday Times* Rich List.

Strictly speaking, New Money Mayfair is more than hedge funds. There are 'private-equity' houses like Permira, Blackstone or Hamilton Bradshaw. They're businesses which acquire other big businesses after pulling apart their accounts in very forensic ways. They analyse their assets and their people and their vulnerabilities like someone intent on a hostile takeover. Then they get the firms to take on a mountain of debt to allow the private equity firm to buy them and transform them. It's brilliant. It's alchemy. Private equity firms own massive tranches of British business now, famous names like Boots and Bookers.

And then, smartest and most secretive of all, there are the 'family offices'. The world has more billionaires than ever – rich people with a few hundred million are pretty common-place – and billionaires have so much *private* business to transact, so many investments, different *asset classes* – art, property, equities – to look after in so many time zones and tax jurisdictions, that the old systems of lawyer, banker, accountant, aren't enough. If you're really rich, you warrant an office with two or three smart ex-bankers and some well-connected girls looking after *everything* from the new shooting estate in Scotland to your teenage son's Ferrari.

An old ex-City friend works for an Arab, doing this stuff – he's still got children in the expensive years at expensive schools. He looks after his employer's family, they look after him. In Mayfair, another friend looks after a roster of the Euro-rich. He and his partners handle fifteen families – the most modest has around two hundred and fifty million pounds of 'investible wealth', the richest has 'a billion plus' – in an office that's so oppressively elegant, with its contemporary art-and-museum-quality everything, that it sets me on edge just waiting five minutes in reception.

The global rich, increasingly, live in Mayfair. The Grosvenor Estate has been returning the best old buildings, ones that were converted to post-war offices, back into grand houses for people who won't spend much time there. The people who look after their money – some of them astonishingly rich too – work there. And a lot of the world's most expensive *objects* are sold there too. The art trade, the jewellery trade. And luxury-brand everything. London sells nearly 20 per cent of the world's 'fine art', the third biggest seller after China and the USA. The largest part of that trade is in Mayfair and St James's. Forget Shoreditch. Art has become another global *asset class*, like Mayfair property. You don't have to know anything or give a toss, because there are people to do it for you. Independent curators like my sublimely elegant supremely connected Euro-friend who will introduce you to artists and dealers or take you on studio visits if you want do the tour (more likely it'll be your wife, the guy from your private office or your decorator; you're out making money).

Mayfair and St James's are absolutely

humming with very superior *butler* types –
many of them well-bred Brits. We've become
very good at looking after the rich. Think
of the butler character in *Arthur*, played
by John Gielgud. Think of Stephen Fry
as Jeeves – all *enabling* away, smoothing the
path. They're earning a very fair whack – as
family-office men, smart estate agents or
super-concierges, like the clever boys in
Ben Elliot's Quintessentially business, or as
frontmen for luxury-goods companies and the
rest – but they're not usually the principals,
the owners, the definably super-rich themselves.
They're *super-help*. The driving force is somewhere
else, usually somewhere offshore.

Mayfair and St James's, on either side of
Piccadilly and served by the two entrances of
Green Park Station, often get bundled together
now. There's a new linking theme between
them: those hedge funds, private equity houses
and 'family offices'. They're the new Money
District, ancient areas, taken over by the global
rich. The fleeter-footed, less corporate global

rich. People with their own and their family's skin in the game.

Dignified and Ancient: St James's

St James's is thick with *Importance* and *Royalty*. The *dignified* rather than the *efficient*. It's more than just anciency, though it is, most of it, pretty old. It makes you feel, in a completely fraudulent way, that your own mission there might be that much more important. 'Important' is the word senior auctioneers like Christie's – their headquarters are in King St, St James's – use for old objects and pictures which are going to be quite stonkingly expensive. 'Important' is, say, a Chippendale (big-*brand*) commode, made originally for a major toff (hence *provenance* and *historic interest*) in a singular design (where craft becomes art) with only one known companion piece (in another grand house or major national collection). 'Important' is a full-length stunna of a late-eighteenth-century beauty in costume, as in *Lady X as Diana the Huntress* by Gainsborough or Reynolds.

'Important' is code for 'You're in a world where million-pound prices are commonplace; are you cool with that?' The Big Art market on either side of Piccadilly *is* important. (Mayfair has Sotheby's and Cork Street; St James's has Christie's and all the dealer streets around it.) The money there is big and getting bigger. The buyers come from *everywhere*. It's increasingly Monopoly-board money, *asset-class money*. It's all about investment now.

Historically Mayfair did modern (starting with Cork Street in the thirties) and St James's was more trad. Jay Jopling's original White Cube Gallery in Mason's Yard has changed all that. The power base of St James's is changing behind the façades.

St James's clubland *looks* important. Pall Mall's row of mid-nineteenth-century palace fronts by Barry and other architectural dependables is meant to impress. Those clubs were built for the expanding upper-middle class of the military and the professions, academics and clerics, many of them pumped up by empire. They're palaces for men who usually didn't have their own.

The full-on toffs clubs – the ones for men who did – are earlier and smaller: White's, the Turf, Boodle's and Brooks's. Everyone's constantly amazed at how the clubs, most of them, keep going. They're maintaining high production values and period drama in buildings worth three thousand pounds a square foot minimum, *as something else*, but they still only seem to look after a few snoozy old coves in massive rooms. The occasional film-location fee and event-hosting payment can't keep them afloat.

The *real* Power Establishment, even back when Henry Fairlie wrote about it in his *Spectator* essay of 1955, wasn't a gang of old Pall Mall clubmen. *Real power went wider*, to the great corporations, to the emerging medialand people, to Americans. But palace-fronted clubland remained tied to the notion of English gentship – an essentially middle- to upper-middle-class English idea with a romantic Victorian and Edwardian history. *And so over.* It's difficult to rework the Pall Mall clubs without the gentish Not in Trade world-view – and the working lives – that drove it. You can't discuss business and share papers in a proper gentlemen's club. So careerists go somewhere else.

I thought about living in St James's. I nearly bought a flat there a couple of years ago. (Piccadilly, south side, come out of Green Park Station, right past the Ritz and right again.) I could've gone to Jermyn Street and Savile Row every day. *I could've been Burlington Bertie.* ('Burlington Bertie' was originally a successful music-hall song of 1900 about a Piccadilly and St James's toff *flâneur* performed by the male impersonator, Vesta Tilley. It's a lost Piccadilly world where 'Everyone knows me, from Smith to Lord Rosebr'y'. But the parody version of 1915 – 'Burlington Bertie from Bow' by William Hargreaves, sung by his wife Ella Shields, in white-tie drag – became truly, epically famous – 'I'm Bert, Bert, I haven't a shirt. But my people are well off, you know.')

The flat I nearly bought was *very* St James's. It was in an Edwardian *chambers* over the shop – art dealers, of course. It had a giant drawing room, smallish kitchen and three medium-sized bedrooms. The owners obviously entertained a lot with hired help – when they weren't in their house in Norfolk or their villa in Tuscany (I don't have either). The main bedroom was overlooked by the back of Christies' King Street auction rooms. These well-connected Brit specialists (Old Masters, important furniture) and their Euro-trash colleagues could look right in from across the narrow street. I found this vaguely disconcerting, but the owners clearly didn't care: they didn't have shutters or nets. It seemed expensive and probably wasn't. I wanted that bit more room and a better outlook; you wouldn't care if you were only there two days a week.

Jermyn Street, round the corner, isn't quite what it was. It never has been. It was a branch of the Shaftesbury Avenue theatre trade, selling the glorious dream of *clubman* taste to club men, Anglophile Belgravia Americans, Hong-Kong millionaires and Home-Counties snobs. New & Lingwood, for instance, made a lot of having a branch in Eton and a bespoke shoe brand, Poulson and Skone. The others let you know, subtly, that top people shopped there because they Knew the Form.

That worrying Victorian idea of *genthood* still hangs heavy in Jermyn Street. Most of the original shops are called X and Y, as in Harvie and Hudson, Turnbull and Asser, Hilditch and Key, and feature dull twenties wood panelling to get the tourists in the mood. The great staples and stalwarts of the *gent's* wardrobe – ladder-stripe shirts, gingham ones in blues and pinks, reassuring retro materials like Sea Island cotton – feature in so many windows you suspect they must all be made in the same factory. This is where you can get every piece of self-consciously archaic *gent's furnishing* – embroidered velvet slippers, smoking jackets, proper morning dress, proper white tie – all delivered in a totally non-ironic, class-correct way, with not a hint of the Shoreditch dressing-up box or the Fabian-fell-walker design tradition. The buyers and sellers are roped together in a conspiracy to carry on as if this fake Wodehouse-y exchange is all perfectly normal. The assistants go home to Bexley and put on their trainers.

Jermyn Street isn't a closed community any more. Some of the biggest operators on the street are relative newcomers, like Thomas Pink, conceived in South Kensington for a younger kind of City Sloane and owned by the French luxury combine LVMH. And some – like T. M. Lewin; the M&S of the Home Counties professional classes – have windows shouting how many shirts you get for a hundred pounds. And there's the odd bling shop like Vincci, selling the kind of 'Italian' looks mainly bought by Middle Easterners (very white trousers, colourful shoes with a lot of applied metal). Multiple retailers and middle-class mail-order houses have flagship shops here – *for the address*.

Jermyn Street's changed but without getting *design* in the process, let alone fashion. If you're peddling the idea that all those 'classic' styles – mostly updated between-war staples – are so ineffably right they emerged with Creation itself, then to introduce *design* would be to let in light on magic. But there *is* cleverness and quality on the Street, working with the importance of small differences. Emmett, up the Piccadilly end, has a sort of Chelsea-buck feel – it started in the King's Road – and much more interesting materials, used in shorter production runs. And Emma Willis, the only woman on the Street, makes better, subtler things for tall toffs.

I've been going to Jermyn Street, the Arcades and Savile Row window-shopping practically since I had pocket money. And all at the same time as I was actually buying *Top of the Pops* clothes from the King's Road – and later from Eurotrash Bond Street. It wasn't just about getting *gravitas* at twenty-two; there was something compelling about it all, not just *quality* (as cheap clothes weren't so good then), but a whole aesthetic that you knew you could rework and recombine for an altogether sharper look. And over the last thirty years a raft of businesses, firms now much larger than any of the old Jermyn Street operators, have run with that idea, pumped up that British vernacular style and those materials. Ralph Lauren, Hackett, Paul Smith – even Tommy Hilfiger – have made international businesses selling a kind of WASPy, vaguely Jermyn Street-y, Anglosphere taste back to the world. As for me, I've got a room stacked with thirty years of Jermyn Street shirts, cords and moleskins now. But I keep going back.

If Jermyn Street sells class-correct taste, then Savile Row, over the other side, in Mayfair, has traditionally sold the social armour-plating of *bespoke tailoring*. There are all those old tailors who claim 'Fifty years on the Row' – old Cockneys, old Greeks, plus the odd young woman working down there in the basement windows. But New Money's utterly changed Savile Row. It's nothing like so self-consciously archaic as Jermyn Street. New Money's brought in fifteen-year overnight successes like Richard James and Oswald Boateng, who started locally from high-design, high-end, ready-to-wear for sharp thirty-somethings in hedge-land and property, marcoms and entertainment, and then went into bespoke because the money was there. Alongside Poole's (established 1806) and Anderson and Sheppard (established 1906), the kinds of tailor with Royal Warrants, there are newcomers like William Hunt, who makes Laurence Llewelyn-Bowen's Jason King revival suits with their bell-end cuffs for around three thousand pounds a pop.

New Money and the money from multiples means much higher rents in Savile Row. It's a hot street with a lot of entrists – and that drives the old operators out, round the corner. The tailors on the Row want to turn their practices into *brands*. They want to create ready-to-wear packages that they can sell into those new Chinese shopping malls. And that means big money; getting new Chinese owners, like Gieves & Hawkes did. The ancient military tailor at No. 1 Savile Row is on its second Hong-Kong Chinese owner, and is now set up with a mass of Asian licences and concessions in both new worlds of boiling money.

The Bling Ghetto

Knightsbridge Tube Station has two entrances, one at the Sloane Street corner and one on the corner of Hans Crescent by the side stairs and escalators entrance to Harrods. It tells you what matters round there – *shopping*. Knightsbridge is something of an Un-English Activity now – a key counter on the global-property Monopoly board and nothing to do with England. In Knightsbridge, properties – not houses or flats, but *properties* – are bought by seriously rich people who aren't concerned to find somewhere to live – they have places everywhere (and London will never be the No.1 place for them compared to Riyadh or Kiev). These non-resident aliens often don't even see the places they buy themselves. The *family-office* guy will do that. If the numbers and the tax things can be done – i.e., if it can be owned in an accommodating off-shore tax jurisdiction, *then it's fine.*

If over a fifteen-year-period, 80 per cent of the *best*, meaning *the most expensive* – irrespective of whether they're beautiful or hideous – places in an area are bought on this basis by those kinds of people, then it changes dramatically. The prevailing tone in Knightsbridge now is silly foreign money. Silly for the size of it, absolutely dwarfing anything home-grown, and silly for the silly things it buys, the awful cartoon-y bling of it all.

Knightsbridge has been *transitioning* for more than twenty-five years. It was a mid-late Victorian infill development *on the park* with an aristocratic and plutocratic mix – dowager marchionesses, brittle plutocrats, old Americans. It had big flats and pretty secondary squares,

67

but nothing with the sheer heft and Cubitt architectural unity of its earlier, grander, neighbour, Belgravia, down the other end of Sloane Street. But twenty-five years ago something approaching haut-bourgeois, local, normal life could be lived in those nice tall narrow houses and big flats.

But there was always *expensive shopping* and, from the early eighties on, a flush feeling. As money returned to Big London and tax rates went down, British New Money – City, advertising, property and retail – reappeared and went shopping. Knightsbridge was brilliantly located, and a familiar national proxy for rich and smart. Especially for out-of-towners.

Then Knightsbridge went global. In 1984 the controversial Egyptian businessman Mohamed Al-Fayed bought Harrods department store. Harrods was always the defining presence of Knightsbridge, for its size and its brand, as London's archetypal high-end department store. (Its neighbour, Harvey Nichols, was younger, more fashionista and, by the nineties, in Hong-Kong Chinese ownership and famous for its role in *Absolutely Fabulous*.) In 1984, however, Harrods was distinctly dull, under-invested and relatively unprofitable.

Al-Fayed hugely expanded Harrods' franchise. Initially he sold it to every aspiring suburb of London and beyond with powerful TV advertising. And then he got airborne, targeting the people he knew, the emerging Middle-East wealth that had started to travel to London – or to flee there – in the seventies. The traditional Harrods role – as *quartermaster* for the settled, couth, *local* rich – was ditched. High-spending New Money – particularly from the Middle East – was the future. That decision, combined with successive waves of Flight Capital and a new, more confident cohort of younger Middle-Easterners (the Saif Gaddafi generation) has made Knightsbridge unrecognizable over the last twenty years.

Knightsbridge has a new OTT image now. The Concours d'Élégance of young Arabs in cartoony hyper-cars – Ferraris, Lamborghinis,

Maybachs, customized Rollers and the rest –
around Harrods, and the New Cafe Society
along the Knightsbridge stretch, with teens
and twenties wearing full-on, luxury-brand
everything out of the store window, became the
style of the area. Knightsbridge went from the
aspirational next step up for the upper-middles
of South Ken to becoming . . . *a bling ghetto*.

As well as completely unaffordable.
Knightsbridge appealed to the biggest, loudest,
most body-guarded-up kind of money (the
Eastern Europeans joined up in the late
nineties). It became big on the map for a mass
of new global money from *everywhere*. Along the
way it's become less attractive to Americans
and Western Europeans who, in any case, were
being wildly outspent.

More recently Knightsbridge has been
defined by an extraordinary *development* – what
people used to call a block of flats – One Hyde
Park, next door to the great 1902 bulk of what
had been the Hyde Park Hotel (bought and
renamed as the Mandarin Oriental Hyde

Park Hotel by a Hong-Kong Chinese hotel group in 1996). One Hyde Park is a new *'business model'* for super-expensive apartments, invented by the Candy Brothers, a pair of young English property developers who Went Global practically from the start. They bought trophy sites (the Knightsbridge one, the Chelsea Barracks, the Middlesex Hospital in Mortimer Street, W1), brought in trophy architects and marketed trophy apartments globally at the newest, biggest money. They charged an extraordinary premium for them – three and four times the price per square foot of neighbouring flats and houses. Then they publicized the sales and the prices.

The architect at One Hyde Park was the global style star Richard Rogers – or at least his practice – but still nobody seemed to like the buildings that much. The interiors were done by the Candys and their own practice in a style that came to be known as the New Knightsbridge Look. Broadly, it's a smarter Dubai Hilton-plus-plus style with a lot of boys'-toys technology – remote-controlled everything, ostentatious security, panic rooms, bomb-proof glazing – and internationally understood branded finishes, furniture and accessories. Known-Value Items like expensive stones and marbles, fancy finishes like macassar ebony and silver leaf. Lots of off-whitey creamy, mushroomy colours in cashmere and velvet, lots of hard surfaces. And *no* antiques, tchotchkes or pictures. (The Candy customers don't reckon that stuff.)

It's just the kind of thing to give the London broadsheet journalists who managed to view it the vapours. They implied it was vulgar, overpriced and *other* (every effort had been made to ensure the owners never met ordinary Brits. Their cars were brought up in a lift from the underground car park. They never touched a pavement). These considerations didn't stop the Ukrainian mining tycoon Rinat Akhmetov paying one hundred and thirty-six million pounds – the most ever paid for an apartment *anywhere* at the time, so the Candy brothers' publicity said – for a double-sized penthouse affair. Apparently he's spending another fifty million on the interior.

Last year a new Knightsbridge hotel, the Bulgari, was opened opposite One Hyde Park by the Italian-jewellery brand Bulgari. Bulgari is popular in Middle Eastern and Asian Big-Money markets. Reviewing the Bulgari's restaurant, A. A. Gill, *The Sunday Times*'s restaurant critic, set the scene by describing Knightsbridge as 'about as prestigious as a multi-storey car park after a tramp's bladder infection convention. The hotel sits obliquely opposite those two blocks of flats that boast they are the most expensive square feet in the world. But what this burb does have is a drug dealer's sensitivity, an adoration of cost without the faintest concept of worth'. He described the Bulgari Hotel's own style as 'post-minimal megalomaniac's mausoleum' and called it 'a laughable temple of waste'. The new Knightsbridge is probably impervious to this sort of thing; the new people – mostly absentees anyway – aren't fretting over British broadsheets. If they *did* hear about it, they'd put it down to jealousy.

Over the course of the nineties, Sloane Street, starting from the Knightsbridge end, became a major shopping street, completely lined with global *luxury-brand* shops. The same shops as in Fifth Avenue, the Champs Elysées in Paris, Serrano in Madrid and the Via Monte Napoleone in Milan. And the twenty-first-century Bond Street. Designer-brand shops from Milan, Paris and New York – very few of them from London. It was fantastic for Sloane Street's grand landlord, the Cadogan Estate, as rentals shot up. Like other parts of Super-Prime Big London, Knightsbridge had achieved *lift-off*, up and away from the rest of the city – let alone the rest of Britain – and into that strange airborne continent that Robert Frank called 'Richistan'.

Design for Living

Bloomsbury is one place where you'd expect
most of the locals to get Lesley Green's
1906 Russell Square Tube Station. They'd
get the design references – a strong Arts &
Crafts undertone with faintly Frenchy top-
notes. They'd get the ox-blood faience tiles,
they'd understand the arched windows above.
Bloomsbury is London's absolute epicentre of
early twentieth-century design understanding,
of visual nuance-getting. There's the huge
presence of London University all around.
There's the LSE further down in Houghton
Street. Then there's the generalized miasma

of the Bloomsbury industry: biographies, films, TV and picture books on Charleston. There's the British Museum, the Architectural Association's school in Bedford Square. There's the cultish Brunswick council block of 1972, gentrifying at a lick, as its former council flats get bought by architects and art directors. It's hectically architectural in every sense. It's very late eighteenth century in its core architecture, the great Bedford Estate squares (Bedford, Bloomsbury, Russell), and the wonderfully long, narrow, sooty, London-brick Gower Street. And it's festering with blue plaques. More than practically anywhere. Many of them for the Bloomsburys, of course.

Towering over it all is Senate House, the University of London's power centre. When it was built in 1936 it was London's second tallest building after St Paul's Cathedral. A curious sort of short skyscraper, a mix of New York and Euro totalitarian. It's by Charles Holden, the star architect of the Piccadilly Line. (It featured in the film of George Orwell's *1984* as the Ministry of Truth. Orwell thought it was *the* visual metaphor for modern repression.) I first thought about living in Bloomsbury in the late eighties. It was central, historic and architecturally delicious. I assumed you'd only got to ask and you'd get a range of grandly seedy first- and second-floor flats in the best squares served up by eager agents. But there seemed only to be one agent, the interestingly named Frank Harris, and he didn't have *anything* like that to sell, because the squares *weren't for people*. They were completely sewn up between London University and other Good Works and *knowledge-industry* institutions. Plus *lawyers*, everywhere. They *couldn't* be privatized, buzzed up. I gave up and went to Marylebone.

But I was looking again in 2011 and by then Bloomsbury had developed a bit of a property market *in one corner*. And a bit of a smart street scene around Lamb's Conduit Street featuring several clothes shops and restaurants suitable for youngish types who've had a design education. The Bloomsbury look is very distinctive, different from the Shoreditch look, its younger art-school cousin, or its more self-consciously rich, sharp, Regency Buckish relation, the New Savile Row style.

The new Lamb's Conduit Street look *for men* – interestingly there's not so much for women – combines a whiff of Fabian fell-walking – strong shoes and thick tweed – with several decades of New Design references. Oliver Spencer at No. 62, for instance, has jackets called 'Navigator' – grey, five buttons, done up to the neck like a character in a Merchant-Ivory film – *Signalman* or *Polzeath* (in davenport green). Folk, over the road, feels that bit Dutch. Just like the original Bloomsburys you feel there's a fair bit for thoughtful girls who are boys who like boys to be girls who do boys like they're girls who do girls like they're boys* *if you get my drift.* There are *waistcoats* – not morning-dress Correct Form or self-consciously flamboyant ones like in Jermyn

* From Blur's single 'Girls and Boys', from their album *Parklife* (1994).

St, but ones in dark, sensible tweeds and checks. Waistcoats for characters played by Mark Gatiss. Or a reader of *The Chap*.

It's a *very* particular style, Bloomsbury 2012, tremendously *niched*, but you've got it all aggregated successfully round here. *And I can hack it*. I can talk design fogey quite convincingly. I know enough to recognize a suppressed pilaster or a Coade-stone overdoor (the John Soane Museum is down off Southampton Row in Lincoln's Inn Fields). I didn't do history of art, let alone architecture or trad garden design, but if you ask me 'Can you feel it?' I'm so there.

Updated fogey design is *comfortable*, reassuring, curiously classless – over-educated, rather than overbred. *And it's quite overwhelmingly Brit*. It doesn't have to be expensive either, because fogeys recognize and cherish what other, less educated eyes overlook. A nice, 1770, Cuban mahogany table with scratches and a wonky leg. An unframed lithograph by one of Frank Pick's Tube-poster artists – Frank Brangwyn or McKnight Kauffer.

Ben Pentreath, architect, is the poster boy for this corner of Bloomsbury. I completely see the point of his smart little shop in delicious 1730s Rugby Street just off the main drag of Lamb's Conduit Street, even though I'm a bit more vulgarly Mayfair Modish by instinct. I like its combination of eighteenth-century vernacular, Eric Ravilious prints and fifties Penguin taste. Ben Pentreath – his Ben Pentreath Ltd website says 'shop', 'inspiration', 'interiors' and 'architecture' on its smartly retro homepage and among his posts are 'To Garsington' and 'House and Garden in the Early Sixties' – seems to be consolidating a particular band of taste. Could he become the Cath Kidston of the design-educated classes? For *Men*. He is an architect and a retailer, a man with an *eye* and several missions in life: one of them, for instance, is to bring back loose rush-matting. This corner of Bloomsbury's mini-boom is built on the fight-back against bankers, bling-aggressive development and boiling globalism. There are practically *no* Middle-Easterners or Russians – and not many breeders either because there's not much in the way of private gardens. Bloomsbury is about design-conscious singletons and Dinkys. Ben Pentreath – and don't judge him too hastily for it – oversees the Prince of Wales's Poundbury development, roundly hated by most architects as pastiche. (Poundbury strikes a blow for Old Vernacular and Ben Pentreath says that it'll wear in nicely, look populated and humanized and altogether better as it ages.)

Pentreath says the dead hand of the university *killed* the rest of Bloomsbury, but Lamb's Conduit Street and the local landlord, the Rugby Estate, have provided that little quantum of solace for people like him. As we sit outside I see a) a friend who runs the design bit at the British Council, b) her architect friend who runs a practice with an interesting name and c) two West End gallerist friends (strictly contemporary) who'd crept away to plot. The following morning I told *my* architects, Steven and Will, I'd been in Lamb's Conduit Street. *'We really like Oliver Spencer',* they say.

Heaven SW7

South Kensington is a deeply reassuring country of the mind. I lived in South Kensington, off the Old Brompton Road – five minutes max from South Ken Station – from 1979 to 1989. Two floors in Cranley Gardens. Originally a classic case of Stagnant Gardens, SW7, 1870-ish stucco, with lots of multiple bell sets, and 'hotels' down the Old Brompton Road end, Cranley Gardens was originally tattier than Onslow Gardens to the East, though architecturally identical. The late William Rushton, the cheery *Private Eye* cartoonist, lived in the Edwardian mansion block above Christie's in Old Brompton Road back then, which should give you a heads-up on the style of the place in the eighties.

I'd bought the flat from the actor David Hemmings, but the whole thing was done through agents. When I eventually met him, a few months later, only thirteen years after his *golden-boy* performance in Antonioni's *Blow-Up* (1966), based on the sixties star photographer David Bailey, the one who *made love daily*, I was shocked to see he'd become Caligula. He was heavy, baggy, so theatrically corrupt-looking, you were almost waiting for him to take the rubber mask off.

Our house was quite a Cut Above at first. Just three big two-floor flats (nobody in London said *duplex* then). Not cut up into tiny flats. A morose bachelor doctor – fabulously untidy – was on the two floors above me. A lady casting director from the films, above that (the first time I went to the Beverly Hills Hotel I found her on one of the pool loungers). But while I was in Cranley Gardens in the later, post-Big Bang eighties, clever developers started making smart two-floor flats for the new banker boys, all fixed up. The show flats were done in Instant New Sloane, with antiques and chintz. Our house looked positively dowdy beside them.

I was still using the Tube, off and on, at the beginning of my South Ken decade. I worked in Westminster by then, behind Victoria Street, in the God and Government quarter, very near where they built the Channel 4 building in Horseferry Road. I'd been terribly excited by the idea of Westminster, but was it ever boring – Victoria Street was just like Croydon: dull shopping, dull corporate headquarters and dull Government buildings, mostly late sixties).

But I loved my ride to St James's Park Station, set in Charles Holden's 1928 London Transport headquarters building. South Ken Station – a first-generation Victorian chuffer station, but refaçaded by Leslie Green in 1906 – had an arcade of real shops, including the Anglo-Persian Carpet Company, which sold serious rugs and carpets. The station was completely woven into Old Brompton

Road life, always faintly tired, never Chelsea- or Belgravia-smart, but never full-on Earl's Court tacky either. It was Tottering-By-Gently country with, even then, a fair few Euro-types around. Thierrys and Hugues with heavy hair. Because of the local population there was something inexplicably clubby about the station, about the relaxed way even the young Sloanes – technically wage-slave commuters in late twentieth-century mass transport – treated it. Girl Sloanes on the Tube – the girls often got off at Green Park to work in the Cork Street galleries or do directors' lunches then – were still the girls who'd given us the first line of the original *Harper's & Queen* Sloane Ranger article, 'Look, Caroline, there's Caroline'.

The whole Sloane world was moving on while I was in South Ken. The Big Bang and those smart flats were pushing them out. Married Sloanes were going South. The pioneers went to Clapham and Battersea – the first seventies/ eighties breeder territories – and then way out into deeper South London. They went to

Wandsworth and beyond, to the very Tooting/
Balham borders. Their children, born in the
late eighties, are, some of them, sharing in
Shoreditch now. If they're lucky, they're in
Pimlico.

Now, South Ken is getting seriously
international and expensive. Mainly because of
the Frogs; it's France's sixth city, or something
like that. Practically every thirty-something
French haut-bourgeois City-banker boy in
London and his missus want to live there
(overflowing to neighbouring Earl's Court and
Pimlico) The sixteenth arrondissement has
decanted to London. They like the 1860s stucco,
the Lycée, the museums. And Bute Street – our
original little street of butchers and bakers and
cheery cheap Thai and Indian restaurants – has
gone bilingual now. And, of course, they like
Christie's South Ken acution rooms on Old
Brompton Road. It's not as expensive as the
St James's global-money auction rooms in King
Street. In South Ken the general Christie's
catalogues still say 'interior' rather than

'important' pictures and furniture. They're nice things for decoration – five to twenty thousand, rather than millions.

Today South Ken seems cleaner and that bit sleeker, and the Euro-trash migration means houses and flats are more seriously expensive too. Polished up. But it's still not exactly *that* buffed or chic. It hasn't changed utterly in the way, say, Notting Hill, has over the same period. It still looks comfortable, familiar, a nice buffer zone between the Global Plutocratic villas in the adjoining Boltons, SW5, or the bankers bought-up reaches of Serious Chelsea and Heavy Kensington, W8. In Heavy Kensington, all the Philimore Estate big houses seem to have been rebuilt for Super-Money types behind the façades (they say all that digging out for swimming pools is affecting the water table there). And it's an aesthetic world away from the full horror of twenty-first-century Knightsbridge.

Terminally Tacky

Earl's Court is hugely well connected. The big old Victorian District Line Tube Station – redesigned by Harry Ford and Leslie Green for the Piccadilly and Brompton opening in 1906 – is practically a terminus in its in own right. South-west London changes there for everywhere. Heathrow, of course, but also the deep Hackett and Boden comfort of Richmond, Ealing and Wimbledon at the ends of the District line too. Lovely upper-middle suburbia. Rugby-loving country.

Earl's Court is world famous for a sort of *Midnight Cowboy* transient tackiness. The picture is of the hopelessly rackety Earl's Court Road, with its ratty little restaurants, and its very historic patterns of immigration – Aussies! Gays! Everyone else! Kangaroo Valley! Leather Lane! (The Australians seem to have gone home, the gays have gone to Southwark.) Earl's Court is for people you can't quite place. Young couples with battered luggage.

Earl's Court *seems* resolutely, almost perversely unimproveable. It looks beyond gentrification, twinned forever with Praed Street in Paddington and Vauxhall Bridge Road, Victoria, in terminus blight. It's a complete con, of course. Earl's Court doesn't *want*, doesn't *need* a moment more gentrification. Just plot its location. SW5 shades into South Ken at around Ashburn Place, where 5 becomes 7. Just up the Earl's Court Road on the smarter east side, it shades into the impossibly expensive cluster of roads with extra big Italianate villas called the Boltons (the Little Boltons, Tregunter Road, etc.). Average house price: fifteen million pounds plus.

'Edgy' Earl's Court borders stonking wealth

and relates directly to the Home Counties'
sunlit uplands and beyond. There isn't an echt
working-class area in sight; you'd have to get
across to Fulham's rough North End Road
for that (more than a mile away). This after
all is where Earl Spencer bought his daughter
Diana a flat, back in 1980. (Coleherne Court,
as you might expect, is now seriously expensive:
average flat price – pushing three million
pounds).

The *Midnight Cowboy* Ratso-ness of the
main drag tells you nothing about the streets
behind: those huge, rather dark Edwardian
mansion blocks, and yet more Italianate-stucco
Kensingtonial houses with big flats – Earl's
Court Square's houses have spectacularly big
rooms.

The smarter Earl's Court residents, a
combination of older haut-Bohemian upper-
middle-class people and their successors,
pioneer Euro-trash bankers, talk up the ratty
multiculti street scene, but they know they're
five minutes from the Lycée and Bute Street.

In other words Earl's Court remains perfectly safe for Earls and their children, though still not as expensive as South Ken. If you've got somewhere nice to go to at the weekend and smart shopping just up the road, why should you care how many bureaux de change and insanitary-looking little restaurants there are round the corner?

If you want to see Earl's Court in action, go to the Troubadour, the Veteran Folk Club on Old Brompton Road. The Troubadour was originally founded in 1954 (they say Dylan played there in the sixties). Its original decoration – early agricultural implements with the Woody Guthrie feel – is wonderfully, assiduously preserved, but you won't see a single old bearded folky there. For the last twelve or so years, since it was carefully rethought by a couple of (good regiment) ex-army marketing men, the Troubadour, like the Firehouse Club in Cromwell Road, has been heaving with cool Sloanes. Have Sam and Dave been there? You *know* they have.

My widowed great-aunts, my grandmother's older sisters, lived together in one of those ratty, tall, Italianate-stucco Earl's Court houses in their final years. I discovered the maple-seed game there at six, sending them helicoptering down from the top floor to the small garden below. In my mind's eye, it's Patrick Hamilton territory, but the truth is I can't remember what they or the house looked like inside, just that *everybody was a bit shuddery about Earl's Court when I asked them.**

One of my Earl's Court spies, the art-gallery owner Jonathan Ross, says I'm being too cynical and that it remains eternally transient. The Australians may have gone and the legendary gay pub, the Coleherne, famous for its leathered-up customers and the row of hustlers outside, may have been replaced with

* And that everyone called them Minnie and Birdie. What *could* Birdie have stood for? But then my grandmother had another older sister who'd gone to live in South Africa called Ada, so what *could* you expect?

a gastro pub, but *there's always a new group*. Many more South-east Asians have arrived, he says, including a cluster of Thai ladyboys who twitter around in the supermarkets.

The historic motor of transients, the great Deco-ish lump of Earl's Court, the exhibition centre and music venue on Warwick Road (I can remember seeing Bowie back there in the seventies) has acted like a railway terminus for years – it's got its own entrance to the Tube station. It's driven the cheap hotels and the little restaurants and the fast food. But now it's under threat. The plan is to demolish everything on the enormous site and replace it with a new development by another star architect, Sir Terry Farrell. *Apartments*, of course, plus shops and restaurants. There'll be multiple operators with the kinds of covenants developers like. So there goes the neighbourhood.

End of the Line – Is this Cockfosters?

One of the great pre-war Cockney comedians Max Miller's (him of the loud check suits) routines went roughly like this:

Lady on the Tube: 'Is this Cockfosters?'
'No, madam, the name is Miller.'

It adds something to a pretty vacant place.

Cockfosters is the Northern end of the Piccadilly Line, technically in the London borough of Barnet and nine miles from the centre. It's another of Charles Holden's thirties Modernist stations, but surprisingly, not much to look at externally – a low, wide, single-storey brick building across the overground railway bridge. There doesn't seem at first to be any there there at Cockfosters. No sign of a town centre, of anything more than a patchy suburban parade and turnings off to the usual kind of twenties-through-thirties semis. But walk down to the right and there's a bit more, a couple of stretches where there's starting to be a sort of proto-Chigwell, *Birds of a Feather* sort of modest luxury. Several quite expensively got-up big hairdressers. Several kitchen and bathroom-fitting shops with glitzy room sets – all with greys and glass and high-shine black. The Essex/New Jersey look. And nice cafés for the Cockfosters' equivalent of Ladies who Lunch. Latter-day Lesley Josephs. From the names and the looks there's a fair bit of Greek/Greek-Cypriot here, and a fair few sleek, prosperous-looking, non-specific brown people too. The local-authority (Barnet) population breakdown identifies roughly nineteen per cent Asian overall in 2007, with Indians roughly nine per cent.

I went into an estate agent. There's just

one pretty girl there, and I'm doing the usual English thing of wondering where her family are from. She explains Cockfosters' sense of impending wealth and glamour. It turns out that Cockfosters prices are a fair bit higher than Oakwood or Southgate, next and next down the line, because Cockfosters is *next to Hadley Wood*. And Hadley Wood, while not exactly Weybridge, is a place for second-tier celebs and entrepreneurs. There are, she says, footballers and all sorts there. Hadley Wood, like Notting Hill or Mayfair, has its own shiny, free property magazine, with a picture of the harbour at Cannes on the front. And a lot of advertising for cosmetic procedures and dental veneering. So Cockfosters is special by proximity. Nadia asks me where *I* live. 'Pimlico! You must go and see my dad. He's the talkative Algerian in Café Mignon on Warwick Way.' She shows me the details of a minute flat; it's in *Betjeman House*.

Uxbridge, at the Western end of the line, is another Charles Holden station that doesn't look much from the street. But *inside* – and I've got the photographs to prove it – the long hall and concourse, the unlikely, set-back, stained-glass windows, the late thirties arcade of shops and the elegant ranks of raw concrete pillars supporting the platform roof could be in Germany or Sweden. It's that good.

Outside, Uxbridge is incredibly mainstream South-east. Unlike Hounslow – too poor, too ethnic – or Cockfosters – too small and odd – it's got the whole range of the retail UK on offer, a high street and a shopping centre. It doesn't warrant a John Lewis, but it's got everything else. It's Anytown South-east, and is even tolerably historic – the odd, marooned-looking Georgian house. The whole thing looks miles more *secure* than any of the hard-scrabble-feeling centres on the Northern extension of the line. I could quite imagine that, say, Sue Barker grew up in one of Uxbridge's nicer roads (she didn't), or one of those TV weather people.

*

Terminal 5 at Heathrow is enormous: the largest free-standing structure in the UK. It's got something of the future-proofed scale and shine of the super-sized steel-and-glass hyper-stations on the Jubilee Line: Southwark and Canada Water. The Piccadilly Line station below fits into it seamlessly – they're part of the same composition. You surface in big stainless-steel lifts, you walk over glassy walkways with views of glass roofs going on forever, held up by great, white-painted, Richard Rogers guy-rope columns – modern flying buttresses that dramatize twenty-first-century engineering and massive stress factors.

Airport terminals are in a global bidding war for scale and shine as national statements. I remember my first sight of the new (2007) Hong Kong airport as looking even bigger and more statement-y than T5 (by another star British architect, Norman Foster, this time.) But even by my modest 'only English' lights T5 is still quite something. And it's nice to know

I can go there any old Saturday morning just to watch the dress codes at the first-class check-in for the nicer destinations (Basle, Phoenix, Cape Town, Tokyo).

Heathrow is where the new population of the Hounslows, (East, Central and West), has arrived over the last thirty to forty years. The Hounslows are amazingly varied. I'd expected mainly Bangladeshis, but all human life is here. Smart old Sikhs with sharply pressed trousers, North Africans, every kind of Eastern European and even a gaggle of what looked like bemused Tibetan grannies. The Hounslows and Heathrow are hugely interdependent. The whole range of casualized contractors, cleaners and caterers, shop assistants, and check-in-desk girls comes from around there. But cabin crew – more aspirational, even now – *probably not.* They could live a little further back. The girls married alive in Baron's Court, the boys sharing in Hammersmith, or off King Street in Hammersmith. Cabin Crew, you see, remain sensitive to the Edwardian middle-class snobberies of London villages and postcodes. They want things nice. Hounslow – any Hounslow – probably feels like a bridge too far for them. The ticket to Dreamland begins, like in 1906, at Hammersmith.

PENGUIN LINES

Choose Your Journey

If you're looking for...

Romantic Encounters

Heads and Straights
by Lucy Wadham
(the Circle line)

Waterloo–City, City–Waterloo
by Leanne Shapton
(the Waterloo & City line)

Tales of Growing Up and Moving On

Heads and Straights
by Lucy Wadham
(the Circle line)

A Good Parcel of English Soil
by Richard Mabey
(the Metropolitan line)

Mind the Child
by Camila Batmanghelidjh and
Kids Company
(the Victoria line)

The 32 Stops
by Danny Dorling
(the Central line)

**Laughter and
Tears**

**Breaking
Boundaries**

Mind the Child
by Camila Batmanghelidjh
and Kids Company
(the Victoria line)

The Blue Riband
by Peter York
(the Piccadilly line)

**A Bit of
Politics**

The 32 Stops
by Danny Dorling
(the Central line)

*A History of Capitalism
According to the Jubilee Line*
by John O'Farrell
(the Jubilee line)

**Musical
Direction**

Heads and Straights
by Lucy Wadham
(the Circle line)

Earthbound
by Paul Morley
(the Bakerloo line)

The Blue Riband
by Peter York
(the Piccadilly line)

*What We Talk About When
We Talk About The Tube*
by John Lanchester
(the District line)

*A Good Parcel of
English Soil*
by Richard Mabey
(the Metropolitan line)

**Tube
Knowledge**

**A Breath of
Fresh Air**

*A Good Parcel of
English Soil*
by Richard Mabey
(the Metropolitan line)

**Design for
Life**

Waterloo – City, City – Waterloo
by Leanne Shapton
(the Waterloo & City line)

Buttoned-Up
by Fantastic Man
(the East London line)

Drift
by Philippe Parreno
(the Hammersmith & City line)